CHECKERBOARD BIOGRAPHY LIBRARY

EXPLORERS

Sacagawea

Kristin Petrie

ABDO
Publishing Company

visit us at
www.abdopublishing.com

Published by ABDO Publishing Company, 4940 Viking Drive, Edina, Minnesota 55435.
Copyright © 2007 by Abdo Consulting Group, Inc. International copyrights reserved in all
countries. No part of this book may be reproduced in any form without written permission
from the publisher. The Checkerboard Library™ is a trademark and logo of ABDO Publishing
Company.

Printed in the United States.

Cover Photos: Corbis, North Wind
Interior Photos: Corbis pp. 5, 15, 19, 23, 27, 29; North Wind pp. 7, 9, 11, 13, 17, 21

Series Coordinator: Heidi M. Dahmes
Editors: Heidi M. Dahmes, Megan M. Gunderson
Art Direction & Cover Design: Neil Klinepier
Interior Design & Maps: Dave Bullen

Library of Congress Cataloging-in-Publication Data

Petrie, Kristin, 1970-
  Sacagawea / Kristin Petrie.
     p. cm. -- (Explorers)
  Includes index.
  ISBN-10 1-59679-749-5
  ISBN-13 978-1-59679-749-9
  1. Sacagawea--Juvenile literature. 2. Lewis and Clark Expedition (1804-1806)--Juvenile
literature. 3. Shoshoni women--Biography--Juvenile literature. 4. Shoshoni Indians--Biography--
Juvenile literature. I. Title II. Series: Petrie, Kristin, 1970- . Explorers.

  F592.7.S123P48 2005
  978.004'974574--dc22

                                                                      2005017504

Contents

Sacagawea

Sacagawea was a Shoshone Native American who became a famous explorer. Between 1805 and 1806, she traveled with the expedition of Meriwether Lewis and William Clark. This was the first organized exploration of northwestern North America.

Before 1803, the United States reached only from the Atlantic Ocean to the Mississippi River. The western half of the Mississippi River **basin** was known as the Louisiana Territory. It was owned by France.

President Thomas Jefferson wanted to know more about the land west of the Mississippi River. So, he hired Lewis and Clark to lead an expedition to this region. Before departing, Lewis and Clark received news that President Jefferson had bought the Louisiana Territory. They would be exploring the newest addition to the United States!

Sacagawea was the only woman on this voyage of discovery. Her presence provided many advantages. She

1271
Polo left for Asia

1295
Polo returned to Italy

1254
Marco Polo born

1275
Polo met Kublai Khan

Sacagawea is also commonly spelled Sacajawea. Her name means "bird woman" in the Hidatsa language.

served as both an interpreter and a guide. She was also a symbol of peace between the natives and the white men. Sacagawea played a modest yet **essential** role in America's expansion.

1460 or 1474
Juan Ponce de León born

1480
Ferdinand Magellan born

1324
Polo died

1475
Vasco Núñez de Balboa born

Lemhi Shoshone

Sacagawea was a Lemhi Shoshone. The Shoshone did not keep written records of births, deaths, or other events. Rather, they shared these occasions through storytelling. So, details of Sacagawea's early life are from stories passed down in this way.

Sacagawea was born in 1786 near today's Lemhi, Idaho. Her Shoshone name was Boinaiv, which means "grass maiden." Sacagawea's father was a tribal chief. Nothing is known about her mother.

The Lemhi Shoshone were a **nomadic** people. The tribe followed the wildlife that kept them fed. Sacagawea traveled many times from the mountains to the **plains.** From this way of life, she became familiar with much of the surrounding territory.

The Shoshone were poor. They had no firearms and few goods for trade. And, they sometimes struggled to find

1500
Balboa joined expedition to South America

1493
Ponce de León joined expedition to New World

1502
Ponce de León became governor of Higüey

**Tepees are portable. So, they allowed the
Shoshone to move easily from place to place.**

food. The tribe's pride lay in its herd of horses. The
Shoshone had acquired these animals from Spanish
explorers.

1508
Ponce de León's first expedition

1514
Ponce de León knighted by King Ferdinand II

1513
Ponce de León's second expedition, discovered Florida and the Gulf Stream; Balboa was the first European to sight the Pacific Ocean

Stolen

In about 1800, Sacagawea's tribe traveled to the **plains** of present-day Montana. There, the tribesmen began their buffalo hunt.

The Shoshone women remained at the camp. They had a lot of work ahead of them. When the men returned, the women would skin the animals and prepare the hides to be made into clothing. And, they would cut and ready the buffalo meat for eating.

Young girls were not involved in this hard work. So, Sacagawea and a friend went to the fields to play and to pick berries. From a distance, the young girls heard a frightening noise. An enemy tribe was attacking their camp! Sacagawea and her friend fled, but it was no use. Members of the Hidatsa tribe captured them as they were crossing a river.

1520
Magellan discovered the Strait of Magellan

1554
Walter Raleigh born

1519
Magellan led expedition to Spice Islands; Balboa died

1521
Ponce de León's third expedition, died in Cuba; Magellan died

Would you know what to do if your home was attacked? Why do you think Sacagawea was captured?

When native tribes acquired horses, buffalo hunting became easier and less dangerous. The hunters were less likely to be trampled by the buffalo herd.

The **captors** brought Sacagawea to their village in today's central North Dakota. This was many miles from her tribe. At this time, she received her Hidatsa name. The young Shoshone would be known as Sacagawea for the rest of her life.

Upon arrival, Sacagawea likely joined a Hidatsa household. There, she could help the women until she found a suitable husband.

The Hidatsa lived differently from the Shoshone. The Shoshone lived in tepees. They moved frequently to follow their food supply. The Hidatsa lived in earth lodges. And they grew much of their food, including corn and squash.

Sacagawea missed her tribe. However, she appreciated the warm huts and the abundant food supply at her new home. She became used to her work and the Hidatsa way of life.

Eventually, Sacagawea met a French-Canadian fur trapper named Toussaint Charbonneau. Charbonneau had been living among the natives. In about 1804, Charbonneau and Sacagawea were married. Soon thereafter, they were expecting their first child.

1580
John Smith born

1585
Raleigh knighted by Queen Elizabeth I

1565
Henry Hudson born

1584–1589
Raleigh sponsored expeditions

The Hidatsa lived in earth lodges similar to this one.

Lewis and Clark

In October 1804, a group of white men traveled near the Hidatsa village where Sacagawea lived. The strangers were led by explorers Meriwether Lewis and William Clark.

The Lewis and Clark expedition members called themselves the Corps of Discovery. The voyagers had journeyed up the Missouri River from a place near St. Louis, Missouri. They intended to travel west until they reached the Pacific Ocean.

Winter was approaching, so the Corps built a camp among a Mandan tribe. The men spent the cold months at this camp, which they called Fort Mandan. The Hidatsa lived just downriver.

Soon, Lewis and Clark met Charbonneau. They hired him as an interpreter for the expedition. They insisted Charbonneau bring Sacagawea along as well.

Lewis and Clark would need horses to help them cross the upcoming mountains. They knew Sacagawea spoke

1595
Raleigh led first expedition

1588
Raleigh helped defeat the Spanish Armada

1606
Smith joined expedition to North America

Shoshone and would be able to help them trade for horses. Sacagawea and Charbonneau moved to Fort Mandan during the winter. In the spring, they would continue west with the expedition.

Clark *(left)* and Lewis *(right)* served together in the U.S. Army. By the time they departed on their expedition, they had gained experience with natives and the wilderness.

 Westward

Sacagawea was thrilled to join the expedition. But she was also nervous. After all, she was about to have a baby. On February 11, 1805, Sacagawea gave birth to Jean-Baptiste. Clark later nicknamed him "Pomp." In the Shoshone language, this means "firstborn."

Just two months later, Sacagawea and Charbonneau packed their bags. On April 7, the Corps resumed its westward journey. The Missouri River had just thawed, and it was still cold. So, Sacagawea bundled her baby and carried him in a **cradleboard** on her back.

The group traveled for a month, covering 15 to 20 miles (24 to 32 km) per day. Sacagawea either walked or rode in a **pirogue**. On May 14, one of the pirogues almost **capsized**. Much of the expedition's notes, maps, and equipment went into the river. Thankfully, Sacagawea rescued everything from floating away. The journey then continued west.

1607
Hudson's first expedition

1609
Hudson's third expedition

1608
Hudson's second expedition

On May 20, the group named a river in Sacagawea's honor. However, today it is known as Crooked Creek. It feeds into the Missouri River.

Despite the difficult travel, Sacagawea never complained. In fact, she made the hard times easier for the voyagers. She found roots and berries for the men to eat. She also showed them how to make clothes and moccasins from leather.

1614
Smith led expedition to North America, charted and named New England

1610–1611
Hudson's last expedition, he died

1616
Raleigh's second expedition

The Great Falls

Throughout the journey, hardly a day passed when everyone was healthy. Sacagawea became very ill, too. Lewis and Clark took turns caring for her. When the voyagers came upon a mineral spring, Lewis made Sacagawea drink the water. He believed the water would heal her.

The group camped for several days near the spring. Then the voyagers resumed their journey. On June 13, the explorers reached the Great Falls of the Missouri River. These falls are more than 90 feet (27 m) high!

The only way around the falls was to walk. So, the men built carts to haul their boats and equipment. Then, Sacagawea and the voyagers **portaged** around the falls. The weather made travel along the steep paths nearly unbearable. At one point, Sacagawea and Pomp were nearly washed away by a flood.

1618
Raleigh died

1637
Jacques Marquette born

1645
Louis Jolliet born

1631
Smith died

1643
René-Robert Cavelier de La Salle born

Would You?

Would you continue with the expedition after nearly being washed away? What other stories do you think Sacagawea shared from the journey?

The group carried its boats and supplies 18 miles (29 km) around the Great Falls. This added an extra month to the journey.

Familiar Sights

Beyond the falls, the explorers returned their boats to the river. On July 25, they reached a place called the Three Forks. There, the Missouri River splits into three smaller rivers. Lewis and Clark named the rivers the Jefferson, the Madison, and the Gallatin. Sacagawea recognized this place. She had been taken from here many years ago.

Lewis and Clark led the group up the Jefferson River. As they approached the Rocky Mountains, Sacagawea recognized more **landmarks**. They were nearing Shoshone territory!

Lewis decided to lead a smaller group ahead to find the Shoshone. Surprisingly, Sacagawea was not included. On August 13, Lewis's group came upon some Shoshone women gathering food. At first, the women were frightened. But, the men offered them gifts. So, the Shoshone welcomed the explorers into their village.

1669
La Salle explored Ohio region

1666
La Salle sailed to Canada

1673
Marquette and Jolliet explored the Mississippi River

Would you want to help lead an expedition? What do you think Sacagawea's biggest contributions were?

Sacagawea did not speak English. However, she still was able to communicate with the voyagers through both sign language and her husband.

Reunion

Meanwhile, Clark's group was slowly traveling by water through Shoshone territory. In mid-August, several natives approached them on horseback. Sacagawea recognized them from a distance. This was her tribe!

The Shoshone men took Sacagawea and the voyagers to their camp. There, the explorers found Lewis and his small party. Sacagawea also reunited with a long-lost friend. But sadly, most of her family had died. Only two brothers and a nephew remained.

Sacagawea's brother Cameahwait had become a tribal chief. After an emotional reunion, Sacagawea explained the mission of the voyagers. She told Cameahwait that the explorers needed horses in order to cross the mountains.

Cameahwait agreed to trade with the white men. This was a good idea for the tribe. The Shoshone were very poor and nearly starving.

1675
Marquette died

1682
La Salle's second Mississippi River expedition

1679
La Salle's first Mississippi River expedition

Even though they were traveling with Sacagawea, Lewis and
Clark knew they needed to calm the suspicions of the Shoshone.
So, they provided gifts such as shirts, tobacco, and meat.

1687
La Salle died

1684
La Salle's third Mississippi River expedition

1700
Jolliet died

The Rockies

Soon, the Shoshone men prepared to leave on a buffalo hunt. Lewis and Clark worried their group would be stranded if the Shoshone left. So far, they had received only three horses.

Lewis talked with Cameahwait, who agreed to provide more horses. In the end, the Corps received 29 horses and a Native American guide named Toby.

In late August, the expedition left the Shoshone camp. It was a sad good-bye for Sacagawea. She would miss her people, but she had a job to do.

The group started north along the Lemhi River. Soon, they began the dangerous passage through the Bitterroot Range of the Rocky Mountains. The climb was miserable. Horses slid off the steep trails. To make matters worse, it snowed on September 3. Everyone was cold, and **game** was scarce.

1770	1786
William Clark born	Sacagawea born

1774	1800
Meriwether Lewis born	Sacagawea captured

The Bitterroot Range is part of the northern Rocky Mountains. The horses that the expedition received from the Shoshone made the journey easier.

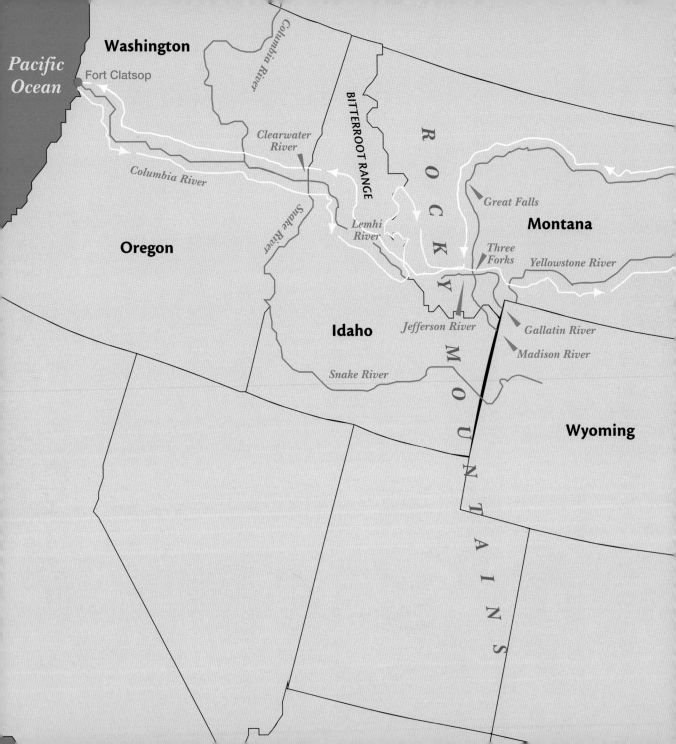

CANADA

N

Missouri River

Fort Mandan

**North
Dakota**

Minnesota

**South
Dakota**

Missouri River

Mississippi River

The Journeys
of Sacagawea

1804 TO 1805 ➡ ————————

1806 ➡ ————————

The Pacific

In mid-September, Sacagawea and the voyagers met members of the Nez Percé tribe along the Clearwater River. The Nez Percé helped the group make dugout canoes. From that point on, the explorers traveled by water.

By following the Clearwater, Snake, and Columbia rivers, the Corps reached Oregon. It soon arrived near the Pacific Ocean. The group built a **stockade** south of present-day Astoria. The explorers spent a rainy winter at Fort Clatsop.

Sacagawea did not see the ocean for some time. Finally, she joined Clark on an outing to see a beached whale. For the first time, she saw the endless body of water. She was amazed that animals as large as this whale filled these waters!

On March 23, 1806, Sacagawea began the return journey with the Corps. The group reached the Hidatsa camp in August. There, Sacagawea and Charbonneau said their

1804
Lewis and Clark began exploring the Pacific Northwest

1806
Lewis and Clark returned to Missouri

1805
Sacagawea joined the Lewis and Clark expedition

good-byes. The rest of the voyagers continued down the Missouri River. Charbonneau received $500 for his efforts. Sacagawea was paid nothing for her priceless work.

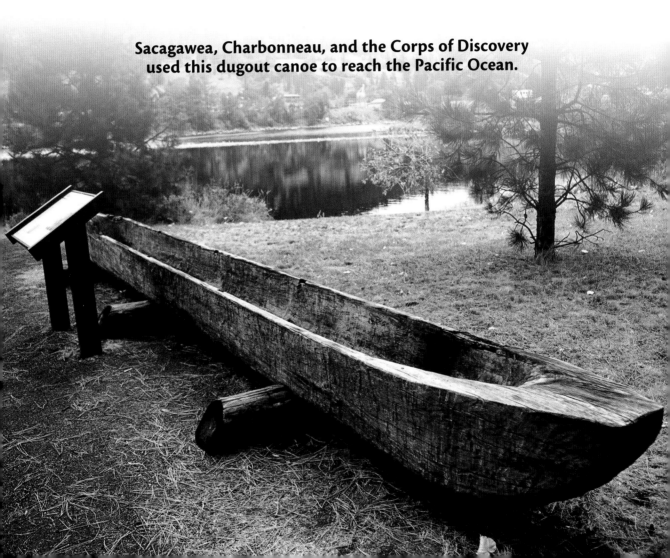

Sacagawea, Charbonneau, and the Corps of Discovery used this dugout canoe to reach the Pacific Ocean.

Moving East

Sometime later, Clark wrote to Charbonneau. He had become very fond of Pomp and Sacagawea. Clark requested permission to care for Pomp and provide him with an education. He offered Charbonneau land and animals if he would bring his family to St. Louis, Missouri.

Charbonneau accepted this invitation. The family moved to St. Louis in 1809. Together, they began a new adventure. However, Charbonneau missed the **plains** and his friends. In 1811, he and Sacagawea left St. Louis while Pomp remained with Clark.

Sacagawea and Charbonneau moved to Fort Manuel in today's South Dakota. There, Sacagawea had a child named Lizette. Soon after Lizette's birth, Sacagawea became ill with a fever. Sacagawea died on December 20, 1812.

Sacagawea was a valuable resource to the Corps of Discovery. Through the group's many hardships, this young

Sacagawea's contribution to America's expansion is honored on the U.S. golden dollar coin. The coin went into circulation in 2000.

woman remained positive and useful. She helped guide the voyagers, feed them, and keep their spirits high. Today, **landmarks**, monuments, and memorials pay respect to Sacagawea.

1893
Peary's first expedition

1909
Peary's third expedition, reached the North Pole

1905
Peary's second expedition

1920
Peary died

Glossary

basin - the entire region of land drained by a river and its tributaries.

capsize - to turn over.

captor - one who has captured a person or a thing.

cradleboard - a flat board used to hold a baby. It could be carried on the mother's back or hung from a tree so that the baby could see what was going on.

essential - very important or necessary.

game - wild animals hunted for food or sport.

landmark - an important structure of historical or physical interest.

nomadic - moving from place to place, usually seasonally, within a well-defined territory.

pirogue - a boat made by hollowing out a large log.

plain - a flat or rolling stretch of land without trees.

portage - the transporting of boats or goods across land from one body of water to another.

stockade - a defensive barrier made up of tall posts, usually forming an enclosure.

Saying It

Hidatsa - hih-DAHT-suh
Jean-Baptiste Charbonneau - zhahn-baw-teest shawr-baw-noh
Lemhi - LEHM-heye
Nez Percé - NEHZ PUHRS
pirogue - PEE-rohg
Shoshone - shuh-SHOHN
Toussaint Charbonneau - too-san shawr-baw-noh

Web Sites

To learn more about Sacagawea, visit ABDO Publishing Company on the World Wide Web at **www.abdopublishing.com**. Web sites about Sacagawea are featured on our Book Links page. These links are routinely monitored and updated to provide the most current information available.

Index